I LOVE ME!

"I was impressed when I read 'I LOVE ME!' by two young and passionate kidpreneurs, Elisha and Elyssa. As a CEO, this book moved me with its practical and personal insights that teach young girls about business and being the best 'you' possible. Elisha and Elyssa have created a powerful book that provides their peers with specific steps they can take to find happiness within and achieve success. I recommend obtaining a copy of this book to add to your kids' bookshelf because it's filled with useful information that every child should know."

—**Denise Morrison**, President and CEO, Campbell Soup Company

❤ ❤ ❤

"Elisha and Elyssa teach kids to play big, live big, and dream big. I encourage you to get more than one copy of this book and share it with every child you know!"

—**T. Harv Eker**, #1 New York Times best-selling Author of *Secrets of the Millionaire Mind*™

❤ ❤ ❤

"Elisha and Elyssa are empowering kids to master assertiveness. Every kid and their parents should read it. I wish I had this information when my son was a teenager and was bullied at school."

—**Marie Diamond**, Global Transformational Leader, Speaker and Author, *Star in The Secret*

❤ ❤ ❤

"I love ME! may be the most important Chicken Soup for the YOUNG SOUL since Chicken Soup itself. We ask all our CEO SPACE family in 140 countries to read this book and to gift copies to at least ten families with children 13 and younger. I love ME! is the future of the leadership of tomorrow."

—**Berny Dohrmann**, Chairman CEOSpace.net,
Author of *Redemption the Cooperation Revolution*

❤ ❤ ❤

"I love Elisha and Elyssa's book I Love ME! The whole book is filled with golden nuggets, that if every child knew them, we would have a better world. What powerful messengers you are - I love that this book is by kids for kids it will make a great mark on the world. You are brilliant, beautiful and bold girls and I celebrate your great work! Keep it up!"

—**Dena Patton**, Co-founder The Girls Rule Foundation
and Brilliant Beautiful and Bold Movement

♥ ♥ ♥

"I was highly impressed with Elisha and Elyssa when we shared the stage at Author 101 University. In I Love ME! these fantastic authors teach kids 7 simple, timely, and powerful steps to help them improve their self-image. As a father, I enjoyed reading their amazing insights, and I support their mission to get children started on a journey of self-development at an early age. I confidently recommend I Love ME! and I know that it will inspire many children not only to increase their self-confidence, but also foster a desire to write, publish, and market a book."

—**Rick Frishman**, Best Selling Author, Publisher and Speaker

♥ ♥ ♥

"Elisha and Elyssa have written the perfect book that I wish I had been able to read when I was a young teen! This powerful little gem of a book will plant the seeds of confidence and ensuing greatness in the young minds that read it! If you love a young teen, give them this book!"

—**Sandra Dee Robinson**, Actress/Speaker/CEO Charisma on Camera Performance Coaching

♥ ♥ ♥

"An incredibly thoughtful, unique, and special gift to help kids build their self-esteem and encourage them to follow their dreams."

—**John Jantsch**, Author of *Duct Tape Marketing*

♥ ♥ ♥

"I highly recommend I Love Me! Self Esteem in 7 Easy Steps, by sisters Elisha and Elyssa to support kid's self esteem and a positive self image. This book is an empowering short-read full of wisdom and wonderful drawings that can teach kids confidence in a fun way. Share the perfect gift for kids so they can love themselves while they become the best version of themselves."

—**Starley Murray**, Celebrity Image Expert & Media Strategist

"In their book, "I Love ME! Self Esteem In 7 Easy Steps", Elisha and Elyssa have created a book that you'll want to share with all the kids in your life! This book teaches kids (big kids, too!) to build a positive self-esteem and follow their dreams. Not only is it great for kids, but also a great resource anyone working with kids that wants to teach them positive core values, self-love, and giving back! As an uncle, I can't wait to share this gift with my nieces and nephews!"

—**Roberto Candelaria**, Author, Consultant, Speaker

"Like the two ladies who created this book, it may be small, but do not let its size fool you. This little book holds a wealth of information intended for the young, but useful to all ages. Elyssa and Elisha have broken down some key concepts, that when utilized and put into action, create a solid foundation for living your best life. They bravely share examples of how they learned some of these lessons in their own life and beautifully illustrate through words and drawings how these lessons change their lives daily. They also share a message dear to me – we are each our own unique design and this is something to be celebrated. I encourage people to read this power packed little book and to share it with children everywhere. It is a timely message that can benefit everyone who reads it. If I had 10 thumbs, they would all be up!"

—**Dianne Burch**, Author of *MaxNificent! The Polka Dot Pyrenees*

"Success is not an accident; it is the result of following principles that take you from where you are to where you want to be. In their book, I Love ME!, Elisha and Elyssa outline 7 principles that each child in the world must learn at a young age in order to achieve success and lasting happiness. I Love ME! is a must buy book for parents encouraging their children to be their BEST within their abilities."

—**Elizabeth McCormick**, Former Black Hawk Pilot, International Motivational Speaker

"I Love ME! Self Esteem In 7 Easy Steps, by sisters Elisha and Elyssa, is an incredibly thoughtful, unique, and special gift to help kids build their self-esteem and encourage them to follow their dreams."

—**David L. Hancock**, Founder of Morgan James Publishing, Chairman of Guerrilla Marketing International, and President of Habitat for Humanity Peninsula and Greater Williamsburg

"I Love ME! is very relatable, encouraging and easy to understand. It will empower your children through Elisha and Elyssa's wisdom and insights, found in every page and story in the book. I honestly think this book should be in the hands of every parent that wants their kids to have a positive attitude. It can teach kids the importance of building self-esteem, self-image and confidence. The positive values the book teaches are truly remarkable. I Love ME! is for kids and parents, by kids for kids, by kids for parents, by kids for everyone who wants to live an inspired and happy life."

—**Veronica Brooks**, International Author Coach and Speaker

"When I met Elisha and Elyssa and learned about their passion to change the world and the lives of millions of kids worldwide, I was immediately on board. I Love ME! is the first non-fiction self-help book for kids written by kids, and it is filled with inspirational stories, age-appropriate wisdom, and fun exercises that any kid would love – and will definitely learn from."

—**Larry Benet**, Chief Connector and Co Founder of SANG and Author of *Connection Currency*

💙 💙 💙

"As the father of two young men, I sometimes wonder what it might have been like to have had daughters. While nothing can replace my boys, if I would have had girls, I could only hope and pray that they would have been as beautiful, intelligent and caring as Elyssa and Elisha. They are truly a gift to us all."

—**Steve Olsher**, New York Times bestselling Author of *What Is Your WHAT? Discover The ONE Amazing Thing You Were Born To Do*

💙 💙 💙

"There is only one way to describe Elisha and Elyssa: OLD SOUL MESSENGERS. Their book 'I Love ME!' is a true reflection of them manifesting their God given gift, which is to empower and equip kids to be their best selves and follow their dreams. The book is thought-provoking, engaging, FUN, interactive and practical. They challenged me to look in the mirror, and ask the question 'Am I doing all I can to love myself, live my purpose and be the best for others?' This book might have been written for kids, but it will change a lot of adults' lives too! Well done, Elisha and Elyssa, the future of the world will be a better place as a result of kids getting your book in their hands!"

—**Lisa Randolph**, CEO, Kaizen Endeavors and Dream Angels, Inc. Mentor

💙 💙 💙

"Oh how I wish I would have known when I was a kid what Elisha and Elyssa teach in their book "I Love ME!" Can you imagine how different the world would be if we all taught our children these things?"

—**Gerald Rogers**, Bestselling Author, Speaker and, most importantly, Dad!

"When I saw Elisha and Elyssa, I knew that there was something special about them as they sat in a conference for women business owners. I watched them confidently engage adults with big, bright smiles. Their confidence was a magnet that drew people to them. I was one of those people. As I watched them, spoke with them and came to know them, I saw then, and now know, that they exemplified what I hope would be possible for all children and teens…They were confident. They were empowered. They want to make a difference in the lives of others, especially other children. I am not surprised that the two of them would write I Love ME. They are the perfect pair to tell a story to children about loving self so that they can give love to others."

—**Coretta Turner**, CEO, 3D Discovery

"I Love ME! Self-Esteem In 7 Simple Steps is a fun, encouraging, inspiring, and educational short read, packed with wisdom and insights for kids by kids."

—**Jill Lublin**, 3x Bestselling Author including
Get Noticed, Get Referrals (McGraw Hill) and International Speaker

"This is a fantastic version of positive learning for young readers. It's a path for our youth to learn personal development and a true gift for personal success principles. Love it is for children by children making it accessible to our future generations! Great work ladies!!!"

—**Shellie Hunt**, CEO/Founder Success is by Design, The Women of Global Change

"Let's face it, we live in a very competitive world where we are easily judged by others. Reading this empowering book will provide your child with key insights that will make themselves continue to feel whole, regardless of their peer's opinions. Don't let their ages of these young media moguls fool you; I Love ME! is a powerful book on self-esteem that should be in every child's library."

—**Richard Krawczyk**, Author of *Ultimate Success Blueprint*, Speaker, Consultant, Philanthropist

❤ ❤ ❤

"Elisha and Elyssa are wonderful sisters. They wrote this book so you can become better. Take it from me, a martial arts master. You'll learn, you'll smile, and start feeling happier. Having met them in person, I know in my heart that these tweens, with the loving support of their family, will do great things in this world. Buy this book, read it with your child/children, and be inspired by its life-affirming message."

—**Master Phil Nguyen**, 7th Degree Black Belt, Author of *9 Secrets to Becoming a Bully Buster*

❤ ❤ ❤

"I Love ME! is a great book for a kid or the kid inside you. Be inspired to live your best life, feel good, go after your dreams and most importantly HAVE FUN. Thank you Elisha & Elyssa!"

—**Sandra Champlain**, Author of the #1 International Bestseller
We Don't Die: A Skeptic's Discovery of Life After Death

❤ ❤ ❤

"I LOVE ME! is an extremely powerful and uplifting inspiration by two lovely young hearts to give kids and tweens an instant shot of self-esteem and timeless truth."

—**Imran Rahman**, Author of *Be More, Do More, Have More:
365 Tips To Living A More Powerful and Purposeful Life*

"When I read I LOVE ME! tears ran down my face. I wish I had an I LOVE ME! book when I was growing up. It's an empowering book by kid-preneurs that not only teaches confidence and self-esteem to kids but also encourages people of all ages to follow their dreams. Elisha and Elyssa's words of wisdom are great reminders for me too. I highly recommend kids, parents, grandparents, teachers and caregivers to read and discuss I LOVE ME! so that we can create a better world."

—**Carol Wain**, The Queen of Reinvention

"I Love ME" book is a great resource not only for kids, but for older kids (adults) as well. I really love the way all 7 steps have action steps at the end of each chapter, because having knowledge of anything is not enough unless and until you take action. Elisha and Elyssa have given great guidance after each chapter to take action and love the key words that they have written at the end of the book. I highly recommend this book for all ages. This is a perfect time to share this book. Very inspiring."

—**Sangita Patel**, Author, Speaker and Holistic practitioner of Embrace Your Inner Self.

"Out of the Mouth of These 2 young girls come Nine Pound Pearls of wisdom that all of us must learn. Our Children need this message so they can be the Change the World longs for right now."

—**Patrick Dougher**, TV Host of DoerTV.com

"In their first book together, 'I Love ME!' sisters Elisha & Elyssa prove that they are two of the top thought leaders of their age. 'I Love ME!' is a brilliant example on how to engage the world in positive change by offering real solutions for young people to learn powerful positive

techniques to live in harmony with themselves and others. These two amazing young ladies bring values, confidence, resources and personal empowerment to people of all ages. I can't wait to see what these girls do next!"

—**Robin Rapture**, Executive Vice President of Friye™,
Speaker/Author and International Champion Cheerleader

"As soon as I met these two young ladies, I knew Elisha and Elyssa were very special. Through their "I Love ME" book they have shared a message that is absolutely invaluable to all kids so that they can have better relationships with themselves and others. I'd venture to say that many adults could learn from their wisdom as well. It truly is a must-read!"

—**Dr. Karen Sherman**, Award-winning Author and
Founder of MakeYourMarriageWorkNow.com.

"I have had the good fortune to meet Elyssa and Elisha and I just love their positive energy and enthusiasm for bringing awareness to this important topic. On top of this, I Love ME! is jam-packed with practical tools, confidence-boosting messages and beautiful illustrations. This is an empowering and inspirational must-read book for both kids and their parents."

—**Trudy Scott**, Food Mood expert, Nutritionist, Author of *The Antianxiety Food Solution*

"Elisha and Elyssa are an unstoppable force, spreading their message of love and self-esteem in a simple, yet powerful way. With their rock solid conviction of who they are, what they are worth, and what they stand for, Elisha and Elyssa inspire children and adults alike to look in the mirror and say, I love me!"

—**Taylor Bare**, CEO and Founder of TaylorMadeWebPresence.com

"Elisha and Elyssa are the sweetest little girls, my princesses, my treasures. I have felt their love and light since before their birth and they have shone bright everyday of their lives. They work hard and play hard. They are passionate, and talented. They are heart-centered and selfless. They are full of gratitude. They are the perfect girls to write I Love ME! because they live it everyday. It is a privilege to be their mom, and an honor to be their home educator. In a world where most kids find heroes in cartoons and role models in celebrities, Elisha and Elyssa have chosen to follow the Christ like attributes of the people they love and trust. Their stories are inspiring, their wisdom is beyond my years, their message is timeless and timely for children and adults alike: know and live your passions, love and nurture yourself unconditionally, be grateful for no reason, and be a cheerful giver. I pray that every child in the world can get access to I Love ME!'s 7 simple steps so they can achieve their true potential, and I applaud Elisha and Elyssa for embarking on this journey to be catalysts and advocates for self-love and lasting happiness, and make a difference in the world."

—**Elayna Fernandez**, Elisha and Elyssa's Mom, ThePositiveMOM.com

I LOVE ME!

Self-Esteem in Seven Easy Steps

Elisha & Elyssa

NEW YORK

I LOVE ME!
Self-Esteem in Seven Easy Steps

Published in New York, New York, by Morgan James Publishing. Morgan James and The Entrepreneurial Publisher are trademarks of Morgan James, LLC. www.MorganJamesPublishing.com

The Morgan James Speakers Group can bring authors to your live event. For more information or to book an event visit The Morgan James Speakers Group at www.TheMorganJamesSpeakersGroup.com.

A **free** eBook edition is available with the purchase of this print book.

CLEARLY PRINT YOUR NAME ABOVE IN UPPER CASE

Instructions to claim your free eBook edition:
1. Download the BitLit app for Android or iOS
2. Write your name in **UPPER CASE** on the line
3. Use the BitLit app to submit a photo
4. Download your eBook to any device

ISBN 978-1-63047-140-8 paperback
ISBN 978-1-63047-141-5 eBook
ISBN 978-1-63047-142-2 hardcover

Cover Design by:
Rachel Lopez
www.r2cdesign.com

Interior Design by:
Bonnie Bushman
bonnie@caboodlegraphics.com

In an effort to support local communities and raise awareness and funds, Morgan James Publishing donates a percentage of all book sales for the life of each book to Habitat for Humanity Peninsula and Greater Williamsburg.

Get involved today, visit
www.MorganJamesBuilds.com

Habitat
for Humanity®
Peninsula and
Greater Williamsburg
Building Partner

Dedication

First of all, I want to dedicate this book to my mom. She was a single mom for eight years, and she has taught me everything I need to know in this world. I couldn't have gotten so far in life without her. I also want to dedicate this book to my little sister, Eliana, because I want her to know she is special just the way she is, and that she can be and do anything her heart desires.

—Elisha

I dedicate this book to all the children in the world that feel no one is there for them and that think they don't deserve to be loved. I want to let you all know that I love you, and I am here to understand you and to teach you. I also want to dedicate this book to my lovely mom, who has taught me so well to be a good example to others, and my sister, Eliana, who I am more than happy to set an example for.

—Elyssa

Elyssa   Elisha

Table Of Contents

Foreword

♥ ♥ ♥

The book you are about to read is special. It's full of empowering tools to help build self-esteem in kids, like inspirational stories, powerful tips and exercises, and fun and colorful illustrations. Yet it is who is behind the book that makes it so special. In a world where many kids focus on how bored they are or what's wrong with their lives, two young girls took it upon themselves to write a book to inspire other kids to be the best they can be. Elisha and Elyssa have their plates full just like most kids: school, chores, extracurricular activities—and they even started their own business. Yet on top of all this, they managed to produce this lovely book to help make a difference in the world. They are an inspiration to kids and adults alike.

I first learned about Elisha and Elyssa's mission a few years ago when I autographed a copy of my book, Beauty's Secret, A Girl's Discovery of Inner Beauty, for them at a conference I was speaking at. I was instantly impressed with the poise and self-confidence these girls possessed, and, in chatting with their mom, I could tell she was actively engaged in nurturing her daughters' self-esteem. The girls soon became faithful subscribers to my empowerment publication for girls, BYOU "Be Your Own You" Magazine, and we even featured Elisha when she applied to be a positive role model for girls. When asked how she will change the world, she answered, "I will teach kids around the world to love who they are." And that is exactly what she and her sister are doing.

Elisha and Elyssa are very fortunate to have had the guidance and nurturing they've had in growing up, but sadly, many kids are not so lucky. Low self-esteem in our children is at an all-time high; our kids are programmed way too early to harshly judge themselves and others. Technology opens the door for daily exposure to unhealthy media messages that consistently challenge a child's self-worth (especially for girls), and bullying can now follow a child home— and in much more severe ways—with negativity increased exponentially behind the anonymity of an electronic screen. Even well-intended parents and educators are challenged in raising kids with positive self-esteem in today's fast-paced world.

That's why the messages in I Love ME! are so important for our kids to hear. Kids with low self-esteem make unwise—and even dangerous—decisions. They miss the joy life has to offer. They suffer from anxiety and unhappiness. And they grow up to be adults suffering with self-worth issues. I know; I was there. I worked for many years as an international model and actress being judged by others, and worse, harshly judging myself. I suffered my own personal, dark journey until I realized I could choose what I thought about myself. I discovered that it is what's inside that counts, and that we are all meant to shine the beautiful light of who we are, each in our own individual way. I've made a commitment to spend the rest of my life making sure children do not allow their light to be dimmed by anyone, including themselves, and to know how amazing they truly are.

I admire Elisha and Elyssa's commitment to do the same. They do a masterful job teaching kids that everyone has unique and special gifts to share with the world. Their stories are personal, their advice is wise beyond their years, and best of all, you can feel the love and authenticity of Elisha and Elyssa radiating from the pages. They care, and it shows. Plus, how cool is it that kids are teaching kids? They truly are trailblazers in the area of self-help for kids. I am proud to support Elisha and Elyssa with their mission to empower other kids. They are a testament that when you teach children to love themselves, to follow their dreams, and invest in ways they can feed their mind positive media, our children can not only thrive in a negative and judgmental society, they can change the world to make it a much better place.

Debra Gano

Debra Gano is the CEO, Publisher, & Founding Editor of the self-esteem publication for girls, BYOU *Be Your Own You* Magazine, and the award-winning author of the *Heartlight Girls* series.

Introduction

Hello!

Our names are Elyssa and Elisha. We are sisters, and as we write this book, we are 9 and 10 years old, respectively. We have a passion to help kids love themselves and care about others. We were motivated to create this book because kids today do not have the resources to think good thoughts about themselves, and they sometimes have very low self-esteem. Self-esteem is the way you think about yourself. Self-esteem is also known as self-image, self-worth, self-regard and confidence.

One of the consequences of low self-esteem is BULLYING. According to statistics, 160,000 students miss school each day for fear of being bullied. In addition, 4 out of 10 children will drop out of school this year because they are being bullied, every seven minutes a kid is bullied and 282,000 students are physically harmed by bullying every month.

Bullying involves hurting a person in some way, either by hitting them or calling them names. You could be a bully or someone could bully you. Think about it. Have you ever been bullied? Have you ever bullied someone else?

Children with low self-esteem might start being bullies, starving themselves or even end up taking their own lives!

We believe this book will help other kids because we have already inspired and set an example for people we know, and we have been able to touch many lives by believing in ourselves. Are you ready to let us help you?

Through our book, we will help you create new experiences, but only by loving yourself will you be able to make them happen. Like religious leader Dieter F. Utchdorf said, "Enjoy the journey!" Take the time to learn the information in this book and don't read it all at once. We want you to be able to use it in your own life and share your love of it with others.

Each chapter has a drawing to illustrate our personal stories. It also includes practical personal insights and exercises to help you be the best "you" possible. Before you start the process, make a plan for how you want to use the lessons you learn here, and then watch everything fall into place.

We hope you learn a lot and that you simply have lots of FUN!

A Note from the Authors

My name is Elisha F. Fernandez, and I am 10 years old. I am in the fifth grade, and I am home-schooled. I used to attend a private school where I was teased about my two front teeth, my good grades (A+ most of the time) and my interests (basketball, volleyball, baseball and reading). All that teasing made me critical of myself and what I looked like, which made me pay more attention to my imperfections than what was in my heart.

My mom taught me that life isn't about being smart or pretty; rather, it's the heart, effort and intentions that matter the most. She always told me, "Don't be afraid to be yourself." This advice has had a huge impact on me and has inspired me very much. Have you ever watched Disney's "The Lion King?" (I'm a Disney fanatic!) Do you remember when Mufasa said to his son, Simba, "Remember, remember, remember who you are"? These words mean that you should remember your true self and not be afraid to show your personality. If only I had paid attention to those simple yet wise words earlier in life! But I know them now, and it's never too late to make a new start!

One of my main reasons for creating this book is to thank my mom for caring for me all by herself for eight long years. She is truly an amazing mom, and I want to inspire other people to love themselves just like she taught me!

♥   ♥   ♥

My name is Elyssa F. Fernandez, and I am 9 years old. I am in the third grade, and I am home-schooled. Like all children (and adults!), I am a child of God. I have always known how to love myself. Thankfully, I have a good mom who has taught me all there is to know about life. Since I have grown up in such a safe and happy environment, I want to thank my mom by changing other people's lives. This is called "paying it forward." My message is that we should all be ourselves and treasure our unique personalities. My motto is: "Don't STRIVE to fit in, be PROUD to stand out!" Keep those words in your heart at all times, and your life will change for the better.

Chapter 1

I Am Loved

"You, yourself, as much as anybody in the entire universe, deserve your love and affection."

—Buddha

My sister, Elyssa, and I are both artists. We have always loved to paint, and because of our passion our mom encouraged us to start an art business named WhollyART. Through our art, we teach concepts like fairness, confidence, affection and choice. We have explored each of these ideas throughout the process of creating works that reflect them. We have always loved participating in art fairs; at some shows, we have even won awards and sold some of our paintings. It is fun to make money and get prizes for doing what you love most!

One day, we were at an art fair at Arts Fifth Avenue in Fort Worth, Texas, where we hoped to sell our artwork. We were admiring our masterpieces when I suddenly asked my sister, "Which one do you think is better, mine or yours?" Elyssa quickly responded, "I think mine is better." I disagreed; I thought my painting was better! We ended up arguing about why we thought each one was better and about why "yours" hadn't sold yet.

After a few minutes of arguing, we decided to ask our mom for her opinion. She answered simply, "I love BOTH of them! They are both special and unique in their own way! I love you both the same, and I will never have a favorite!" Elyssa and I both said "I am sorry" to each other. Then we hugged and started saying good things about each other's work.

This experience taught us that we should not brag or compare ourselves to each other because we all have different talents, and God wants us to focus on what we do have instead of what we don't. We each have our own special talents.

You are like no other person in the whole world! Did you know that no two people are the same? You are special and beautiful no matter the color of your skin, eyes or hair. It does not matter if you are small, medium or large. Nothing about you is a mistake; you were made exactly how you are because your destiny is unique!

No matter what you look like, you are wonderful the way you are! If you are yourself, you will stand out and others will look up to you because you love yourself. No matter what you like or dislike, you are exactly how you are supposed to be. Always think about how you are loved, and you will feel even more love come into your heart.

Keep In Mind:

Instead of striving to fit in, be proud to stand out!

3 Ways You Can Love Yourself More

💜 Stand in front of a mirror every day and say to yourself: "I am loved, I matter, I love myself!"

💜 Pay a compliment to someone at least once a day. When you appreciate others, you will be able to appreciate yourself more.

💜 Find an empty jar (we believe in repurposing!) and name it your Thought Tracker. Whenever you think a negative thought about yourself, write it on a piece of paper and put it in the jar. From time to time, ask a trusted adult to help you burn the pieces of paper to release all that negativity.

Now it's your turn!

3 Ways I Will Love Myself More

1.

2.

3.

Chapter 2
I Take Care of Me

"Your body is a temple, but only if you treat it as one."
—Astrid Alauda

5

My sister Elisha has long straight hair. I've always had shorter, curly locks, which can be hard to manage. One night before my bedtime, my mom asked me to take a shower and wash my hair. So all by myself, I detangled my curls by combing my hair after I made sure the shampoo was all rinsed out. I put on nice smelling lotions, cleaned my ears, brushed my teeth and put away my clothes. I felt very good about myself. Not only was my family proud of me, but I was proud of myself, too. Best of all, I felt that God was proud of me!

You can find many ways to take care of yourself. When you take care of yourself, your spirit feels great and you can do better at other tasks. If you take care of yourself, other people will follow your example. Besides taking care of yourself by showering and proper grooming, you can also take care of your clothing, toys, books and even your shoes. Every day when you wake up, you can stretch to get all the tiredness out. You can dress appropriately in clothes that cover your shoulders, knees and stomach. In addition, you should always do your part in keeping your home clean by picking up your room and putting things back where they belong.

Other ways of practicing self-care include eating healthy foods (even Brussels sprouts and broccoli!), exercising (sit-ups, jumping rope, etc.) and feeding your brain good information (like reading a book about manners instead of a fairy tale).

You can take care of yourself by yourself! When you do things by yourself, it makes you feel good about yourself. This is called self-confidence. Don't worry about always making someone else happy. Take care of yourself because you love your body and want to make yourself happy!

We feel good when we do things that matter, like taking care of ourselves and leaving the not-so-important things for another time. When you need to get a job done but you don't want to do it and decide to do it later, it is called procrastination. This is a trap to avoid because you will never do what you put off!

Life might seem like it will last a long time, but you only have one life to live here on earth. You should want to make the most of it. Even the small things you do count!

Keep In Mind:

When you take care of yourself first, then you are able to take care of others.

3 Ways You Can Take Care of Yourself

💜 Say to yourself every day: "When I take care of myself, I feel better about me!"

💜 Make a list of the things you need to do to take care of yourself every day and hang it in your bathroom. This will be a reminder to take care of your body.

💜 Choose good snacks no matter where you are so you can feel happy and healthy. Even if you don't like a food, you can always find ways to make it taste good, like dipping carrots in peanut butter instead of ranch dressing. Yum!

Now it's your turn!

3 Ways I Will Take Care of Me

1.

2.

3.

Chapter 3
I Choose Well

"To live is to choose. But to choose well, you must know who you are and what you stand for, where you want to go and why you want to get there."
—Kofi Annan

We lived in Florida for seven years before we moved to Texas where we live now. Our mom worked at home and through her efforts, even as a single mom, she has been able to afford to take us to parks and museums. We are always going on an adventure with her! One of our favorite places to visit is Orlando because of SeaWorld, Disney World and the fun museums where we can zoom back into history. We know that most kids don't get those privileges, and we feel very blessed to spend so much time with our mom, to be home-schooled and to always be having fun.

One gorgeous sunny day, we were at Warbird Adventures at the Kissimmee Gateway Airport. We were just looking around in the gift shop, when I suddenly saw a fluffy brown teddy bear with a pilot outfit and the cutest goggles. He was the last one on the shelf!

I told my mom I wanted him. She said that she wouldn't buy him for me, but she suggested I take a picture to have a memory of him. Instead of understanding that my mom had already spent a lot of money and letting it go, I threw a temper tantrum and started crying. My mom then patiently let me choose between the bear and a helicopter ride. She warned me that I would soon outgrow the stuffed toy and assured me that I would enjoy the helicopter ride more. "Are you sure you want to get it?" she asked me. I knew I had a choice, yet I still told her, "Yes, Mommy, I'm sure I want it." I felt I had made a terrible mistake when I waited on the green bench and watched my sister and mom fly above me. I knew that I could get a teddy bear anytime but going on a helicopter ride does not happen every day. I now know that I can choose what I know is right before it is too late to ever have that choice again. Our life is made up of the choices we make, and we learn and grow through them.

We all get to choose for ourselves; nobody makes us do anything. We must not blame others for the things we do or say. We all learn from our mistakes because we realize what to do and what not to do the next time. You can start thinking about whether your choices are good for you and the people around you. To help you understand this better, there are five types of choices you can make: worse, bad, good, better and best. Instead of regretting that you've made bad choices in the past, just make sure the next time you need to make a choice, you rate it to see which type it is. You will find that you'll be making BEST choices in no time!

Everything you choose has a CONSEQUENCE—a result that you get for making a certain choice (an unpleasant result for a bad choice or a reward for a good choice). By choosing the BEST choice, you can feel good about yourself. As a bonus, good choices will inspire others to respect you more!

For example, you can choose to be safe by wearing your seat belt and not talking to strangers. Always choose the BEST choice because you care about your own happiness, as well as the happiness of others. Don't just base your choices on wanting to avoid the bad consequences or wanting to get a treat or privilege from your parents.

We have a method for making choices called S.T.O.P. In this acronym, S stands for STOP, T stands for THINK, O stands for OPTIONS and P stands for PRIORITY. First, you Stop and Think for a moment about your different choices, or Options, and about their consequences. Then you think about your Priority, or what you are dedicated to and what matters most to you. Since my sister and I are Christians, God is our top priority. This means that His commandments are important to us. When you consider your priority and think about what would help that priority grow stronger, you will be happier with your choices.

If you want to become better at choosing well, you must change your thoughts first. Your thoughts reflect your feelings, and your feelings decide what actions you should take. Your actions tell other people who you are. It is never too late to change your thoughts and make the right choices! Choose what YOU think is best for yourself and everyone involved.

When somebody tells you that you should do something, look for the reason why and what would be best for everyone, then make your choice. For example, if your cousin tells you to steal a candy bar because she thinks it would make you look "cool," think about the consequences of stealing the candy bar, how you would feel and if it would make you happy. Some possible results of stealing are going to jail, being banned from the store, not being trusted around other people's things, feeling guilty and bad about yourself, and losing privileges.

Think before you choose, act, speak and write, and you will be happier, smarter and cooler!

Keep In Mind:

Remember to use the S.T.O.P. method to always choose well.

3 Ways You Can Choose Well

💜 Always say to yourself: "I have the power to choose. I will use this power for good!"

💜 Know and accept the consequences of your choices so you can decide to choose better the next time.

💜 Choose the BEST choice even if no one else is doing it!

Now it's your turn!

3 Ways I Will Choose Well

1.

2.

3.

Chapter 4
I Am Grateful

"Some people grumble that roses have thorns; I am grateful that thorns have roses."
—Jean-Baptiste Alphonse Karr

After a very fun vacation at SeaWorld in San Antonio, we were on our way back home on a lovely Sunday evening. We love road trips, and it takes about six hours to drive from San Antonio to Dallas. We stopped at a gas station because we needed to use the restroom. Then we noticed a dog that looked like she'd had puppies. She looked like she hadn't eaten for days. Do you love dogs? We don't have pets in our home, but we love all animals!

We had nothing in our car for her to eat but apples. We rolled one to her, but she didn't even look at it, let alone eat it! Then we poured some water on a disposable plate, and she drank some of it gratefully, but she still looked very disappointed that she didn't have any food.

We usually don't shop on Sundays to keep the day holy, but we decided to make an exception. We bought her some beans, sausages, tuna and, as a special treat, some beef jerky (we are vegan, but we figured she wasn't!). Mom opened the cans and cut up the sausages for her. She ate until every last piece was gone and even came back to lick up the leftovers! We decided to name her Charity because charity means to give help, service and love to someone in need. Charity had a smile of gratitude on her face. It was wonderful to see her attitude change because of what she'd received.

We learned that we can always be grateful for anything that we are given, even if we don't like it. That is the true meaning of gratitude. No matter who you are, where you are, what time it is or how you are feeling, you can find so many things to be grateful for just by looking around you!

We can be grateful for our clothes, food and shelter, in addition to things that do not have a price tag, such as family, friends, hugs, kisses and smiles. Those are some of the greatest things you can be grateful for! Think about it—just the fact that you are alive means you have something to be grateful for!

Remember to say "thank you" whenever someone does something nice for you or when you notice something good that has already happened in your life. We can always take the time to thank the people that take care of us by doing something nice for them without expecting anything in return.

When we focus on the things we have instead of the things that we want, we can be more grateful. For example, if you are at a store grumbling about a toy you really want, you could be grateful for the toys you already have that other kids do not.

You can also be grateful for who you are, your talents and your personality. My sister and I always pray to God to thank Him for who we are. For example, if you really like a famous celebrity, but you criticize yourself because you think you are not as pretty or handsome, you can be grateful you are kind, sweet, loving and good-looking in a unique and different way.

We can also be grateful for the beauty that surrounds us by going outside every day and taking time to be in tune with nature.

A game that we made up, called the "Rainbow in the Clouds" game, will help you remember to be grateful. The clouds represent the things that seem to go wrong in life, and the rainbows represent the things you can be grateful for. You are supposed to think of a cloud and then think of a rainbow that can help you replace the cloud. You can play by yourself or with a friend.

Keep In Mind:

Play the "Rainbow in the Clouds" game to remind you to be grateful!

3 Ways You Can Practice Gratitude

💜 Say "thank you" to someone once a day, even if it is for something small. After you do, reward yourself with a "Gratitude Dance" (a made-up silly dance you enjoy).

💜 Make a gratitude rock. Find a special rock and clean it. Paint "I Am Grateful," "Thank You" or "Gratitude" on it. Put it in a place you can see it often. Every time you look at it, think of something you are grateful for.

💜 Find a notebook or notepad, and write down three things you are grateful for every day. This will be your "Gratitude Journal." Read it whenever you are feeling sad or angry so you remember that you can still be grateful even when you have those feelings.

Now it's your turn!

3 Ways I Will Practice Gratitude

1.

2.

3.

Chapter 5
I Believe In Me

"If you keep on believing, the dreams that you wish will come true."
—Cinderella

Our mom has always told us that we can be anything we want to be if we believe in ourselves. My sister and I wanted to start an art business because we had—and still have—a strong passion for painting. We didn't believe that kids could run a business or that we had a realistic goal to start our own. Our mom kept encouraging us, but we kept on making excuses that we didn't know how to make it happen. Finally, we decided to follow our dream and create WhollyART (with help from our mom, of course!). We have learned that when you make a choice and follow it with faith, anything can happen. When you put effort into making your dreams come true, you can really do and be anything you want!

What is your dream?

Start believing you can make your dreams come true. Make a plan, do your research and then get to work to make it happen!

Remember how I said we love all animals? We once saw a turtle on the side of the road. Our mom said, "Stop the car," and our dad hit the brakes to avoid hitting it. "Hope The Turtle," as we named her, was very hot and dry from the sun. She even had acid dried on her shell! My mom held her on the front seat, and we all said encouraging words to her while she was in our car. Our dad drove to the nearest pond where we left her so she could be safe. Whenever we walk by that pond and see the turtles, even little baby ones, we imagine that it is Hope and her family.

I tell you this story because I believe that it represents our lives. We have to believe in ourselves to cross the road, or meet our challenges, and we have to accept help when we need it, like when we helped Hope get back to the pond. We not only need to believe, we must take action and that first step for wishes to come true.

Sometimes we feel like we can't achieve our dreams because they seem so far away. But sometimes you are so close to reaching them that you just need to believe and have faith!

One of my favorite field trips when I lived in Florida was going to Thomas Edison's home and seeing his inventions. Did you know that his own teacher told him that he wasn't smart because he asked too many questions? His mom home-schooled him for this reason, and Thomas Edison became the first person to make a light bulb! It doesn't matter what anyone thinks of you ... you are smart and you can do anything you BELIEVE you can do.

When you have a dream, be patient and have DETERMINATION to achieve your dream. Keep thinking you can do it even if people tease you. They cannot change your destiny—only YOU can.

When you begin a project, you have to complete it if you want to get somewhere in life! You have the talent and intelligence for what you are destined to do. If you just put effort into your dreams and if you have faith, you can do anything. So keep holding on to your dreams and don't ever give up! I recommend that instead of focusing on the reasons why you can't do something, you start focusing on all the reasons why you can do something.

If people tell you your dream is worthless, keep working to achieve your dream, even when it is not easy. Ignore the negative things people say. If you have faith along the path of your dreams, you will get ALL you are expecting.

But remember, while you are waiting for your dreams to come true, be sure to enjoy what is happening around you. You don't have to wait for the future to be happy!

Keep In Mind:

No dream is ever too big or too small. What matters is that you believe in it regardless of what other people think.

3 Ways You Can Have More Faith In Yourself

♥ Close your eyes and say to yourself: "This is possible. If I can believe it, I can achieve it!"

♥ Make a dream board. Cut out pictures of what you want to have and who you want to be, and put them on a piece of poster board. Look at your dream board every day, and imagine yourself having and becoming what you desire.

♥ Choose friends that believe in themselves. Try as hard as you can to stay away from negative people who don't have confidence in themselves or in you.

Now it's your turn!

3 Ways I Will Have More Faith in Myself

1.

2.

3.

Chapter 6
I Can Be More

"Whether you think you can, or you think you can't—you're right."
—Henry Ford

lisha and I love music. We sing in the church choir, play the guitar and piano, and take voice lessons. One afternoon, I was practicing the song "Shepherd's Flute" on the piano, and I was frustrated. I thought I "couldn't get it right." I was thinking bad thoughts about myself, and I burst into tears. When my mom heard how upset I was, she called me into her room. I tried explaining that I couldn't do it right, but my mom didn't want to hear that. She pretended to play the song, and it was funny.

I realized even if I wasn't as good as other people, I was still better than my mom! I smiled even bigger when she told me that in 10 years, she still would not be able to play the piano because she doesn't practice it. She told me that I still have a lot of time to practice that song, and she said to keep practicing so that I could play the song better. I took a deep breath, and then I went back to the piano. I got rid of the bad thoughts and started thinking good things about myself. As soon as I released the bad thoughts, I could concentrate and get better. After a few more tries, I got the whole song right!

Sometimes we feel like we aren't the best and that we should be like someone else. But by thinking that, we are letting that negative voice in our head take over. Thinking negatively limits your chances for trying new things and making new friends. Avoid people who try to destroy your personality and "friends" who tell you to do things that are wrong, like stealing, lying or bullying someone.

You can always get better at something by practicing, but you should not feel as if you need to be like other people who are "cool" or "popular." You don't have to be like the others and "fit in." Remember what Dr. Seuss said in Happy Birthday To You!:

"Today you are You, that is truer than true. There is no one alive who is Youer than You."

Do the best you can and that will always be enough! You can be better little by little; you just need to practice, practice and practice some more. Do not judge yourself by what others say. It is what you think about yourself that really matters!

Keep In Mind:

Don't doubt yourself, and don't stop yourself. It is never too late to get better!

3 Ways You Can Be More

💜 Always say to yourself: "Practice and Persistence makes Progress!"

💜 Make a list of qualities you would like to develop. What small actions can you take to improve yourself today?

💜 Good books, friends and music, as well as a positive environment, help you be your best self.

Now it's your turn!

3 Ways I Can Be More

1.

2.

3.

Chapter 7
I Give Back

"It's not how much we give but how much love we put into giving."
—Mother Teresa

It was a warm Christmas Day in Immokalee, Florida. We were volunteering for the Northside Naples Kiwanis Club to help parents and kids get things they needed like food, clothes and blankets. Someone dressed as Santa Claus was giving toys to all the kids, and we were handing out loaves of freshly baked bread. Even though our feet were sore and we wanted to go home, we felt so blessed to be able to give our time and love to help those in need. We even made some new friends!

On the ride back to our home in Naples, we cried tears of happiness because we were so touched to be able to do something kind for others! We treasure those moments in our heart. When you give with gratitude and love, it is really giving. When you do kind things for others, you feel good about yourself, too.

Besides the tradition to give back on Christmas Day, we also go to senior resident homes every Valentine's Day. We bring homemade cards, and give smiles and hugs. Even when you don't have a lot to give, when you respect others and give them a smile and kind word, you can make a big difference. Being a good friend by listening to other people's thoughts and opinions is a gift you can always give, too!

Being kind to others is a way to strengthen your relationships with your family and friends. Even though you should be careful around strangers, you can still be polite, respectful and nice to people you do not know. For example, Elyssa and I had the amazing opportunity to go on the Disney Cruise because my mom is a popular blogger. During a stop in Mexico, we got a bag full of candy from a piñata, and we gave it to all the people on the tour bus because we don't eat candy.

Give because you want to make others happy and don't expect anything in return. We can help out everywhere, but we must do it with a good attitude. Don't always wonder, "What can I get?" Instead ask, "What can I give?"

Keep In Mind:

Smile while you are giving, and you will make others smile, too!

3 Ways You Can Give Back With Love

♥ Share your talent and time—not only things—to make others happy!

♥ Make a "Giving Box" and fill it with things you don't need anymore. Pass it along for others to fill, and when it is full you can donate the items.

♥ Pick up litter and put it in the trash or recycling bin to show you care for the environment.

Now it's your turn!

3 Ways I Will Give Back with Love

1.

2.

3.

Final Thoughts

ongratulations! You have completed the seven steps to loving yourself. But this is only the beginning! "What do you mean?" you may ask. This is the beginning of planting the seeds for future growth and potential. This final section is dedicated to giving you tips on how to take the information you've read and make it a part of your daily life.

First, here are some key words to remember:

Affection: a quality or feeling of liking and caring for another

Blessed: feeling successful and happy

Challenge: something hard to do, an obstacle (climbing the Great Wall of China!)

Charity: sharing with the poor and giving love to others (donating clothes and toys, giving or collecting money, etc.)

Consequence: a result or effect that comes from a choice (choice: eating too much candy; consequence: getting a stomachache!)

Determination: doing something no matter what someone else says and no matter what happens

Doubt: to be uncertain about something or lack confidence in someone (doubting you can do a handstand)

Focus: performing a task one step at a time before moving on to another project (finishing your homeless shelter project before holding a bake sale.)

Gratitude: being thankful for yourself and others (Thank You cards, Thanksgiving Day, etc.)

Knowledge: understanding, information or something learned

Opinions: judgments about a person, thing or belief (Two people ride a roller coaster. After the ride, one says, "That was terrific, let's go again!" The other says, "No, let's not! It was terrifying! I would rather go on the Ferris Wheel.")

Options: something that can be chosen, or the power and right to choose (picking out a new toy or book)

Passion: loving something strongly (reading, painting, eating or even sleeping!)

Persistence: continuing, existing or acting for a long time (continuing your business even when no one is buying from you)

Priority: a project or choice that is put ahead of another (chores before reading!)

Process: a continuing action or series of actions, steps or procedures (how to bake a cherry pie)

Procrastination: to keep putting off something that is supposed to be done (watching TV instead of doing homework)

Progress: moving towards a goal, advancement

Respect: concern for other people, caring about others

Self-Confidence: a feeling of trust, belief and certainty in yourself (like speaking up when someone bullies you or a friend)

Selfish: thinking only about yourself and not others (like snatching a toy from your sibling or friend)

Now that you have learned some new words to help you understand this book better, let's move on to some tips on how to better live the lessons you learned.

In Chapter 1, we learned that we all have special talents, but what do you do if you don't know what they are? You can discover your talents by exploring your interests and practicing what you are good at.

In Chapter 2, we learned that we need to take care of our belongings, put away our clothes and keep our rooms clean. We also should be respectful of our books and toys, and always put them away where they belong.

In Chapter 3, we learned that we must think before we choose, and we should always consider how our choices will affect others. If your choice doesn't help you or someone else, then you know to make a different one. You must think about what is most important to you when you are faced with a choice.

You must choose well because you care about your own happiness and the well-being of others.

In Chapter 4, we learned that we can be grateful for things that don't cost money. We can show gratitude for our families by setting a good example for our brothers or sisters. We should be especially thankful for the people who take care of us, like our parents and grandparents, even if they don't always set a good example. We can show gratitude for all the people in our lives by doing something kind for them and not expecting anything in return.

In Chapter 5, we learned that we need to keep trying and believing in order to make something happen. When you believe in yourself, anything is possible. When you believe in what you are doing, you feel like there are no accidents or failures—just results! Remember when we were talking about Thomas Edison? He didn't give up on his dream just because his teacher said he wasn't smart. If you don't listen to the negative comments of others, then you will always reach your dreams!

In Chapter 6, we learned that if you practice (and practice some more!), you can always get better. Maybe you have heard the saying "practice makes perfect," but nobody is perfect, so we made up our own version—"Practice and Persistence makes Progress." That means that when you practice something over and over again, you can get better and better at it! Thomas Edison actually tried 1,999 times to get the light bulb right. At try number 2,000, he succeeded!

And in Chapter 7, we learned that even when you have few material goods to share, you can still give a lot through your words and actions. Think about what a person likes—their hobbies and interests—and that person will appreciate your gifts even more. You could also give something to people who aren't nice to you, and they may want to be kind to you in return. But don't expect a reward; always just do a good deed to be kind.

In each chapter, we suggested three things you can do to follow the seven steps to love yourself. Hopefully, you came up with some additional ideas of your own! Now you can write them down on the next pages in the form of affirmations. Affirmations are positive sentences you write and say about yourself. I am loved, I take care of myself, I am grateful, I believe in myself, I can be more and I give back are all examples of positive affirmations.

I Love ME Affirmations

1.

2.

3.

4.

5.

6.

7.

8.

9.

10.

11.

12.

13.

14.

15.

16.

17.

18.

19.

20.

21.

To sum up our story, we came up with an acronym to share how we can make this world a better place.

We can:

S hine

T ogether by

A cknowledging and

R especting ourselves and each other!

We can all be a **S.T.A.R.** starting right now! Thank you for taking the time to read our book. We hope you will use this information to make great changes in your life!

Acknowledgments

First of all, we would like to thank God, and His son, Jesus Christ, for making this possible. He has given us the desire and the mission to help other children around the world, has put many people into our lives that have helped us, and all the resources we needed to publish our first book together.

Huge thank you to our mom, Elayna Fernandez, for raising us by herself for eight years. Thank you mom for homeschooling us, for cooking homemade vegan meals, for our dolls and our books, for birthing our new sister, and for teaching us to love others and ourselves. Our mom has been very sweet, kind, and supportive, and has mentored us and guided us through each step of our book journey. (We could ramble on and on and on about our mom, but we'll stop here. LOL)

We are grateful to have the most adorable baby sister in the world, Eliana. She has been our inspiration to finish our book even before she was born, and she makes us laugh every day.

Gracias to our familia: Mama Isbelia, Timmy, Elaury, Eniel, Emely, Eleyrin, Papa Milciades and Miriam, Maileny, Karinee, Felicita, Rita, Modesta, and Marianela, for supporting us, and for loving us always.

Thank you to our dad, Taylor Bare, for being kind and gentle, and for all his support, and also to Xoe.

We are thankful for the memory of Papa Manuel, Jay Conrad Levinson, Mama Lidia, Grandma Freitas, Mama Ramona, and many other special souls that have touched our hearts and continue to inspire us.

We couldn't have published this book without the help of our biggest supporters and advisors, Roberto Candelaria, and Audrey Hagen, who have been our angels since the first day we met them.

We are thankful for our best buddies at OfficeMax, (especially Pam!) and for Elizabeth McCormick, for their amazing kindness, for believing in our book, and for partnering with us to save the lives of children who suffer from the effects of low self-esteem.

Thank you to our friends and contributors: Ivan Peguero, Nancy Sustersic, Leslie Knight, Melissandra Barrera, Katie and Brian Willey, Lacy Kirkland, Benson Agbortogo, Robin Rapture, and everyone who made our crowd-funding campaign a success!

We have a big list of helpful experts to thank, including: Jack Canfield, T. Harv Eker, Janet Bray Attwood, Brian Tracy, CEO Denise Richardson, Larry Benet, Steve Olsher, Veronica Brooks, Jeannie Levinson, Carol Wain, Starley Murray, Lisa MacCarthy, Arvee Robinson, Tom Antion, Richard Krawczyk, Shellie Hunt, Master Phil Nguyen, Sandra Champlain, Sangita Patel, Coretta Turner, Lisa Randolph, Christine Malone, Dena Patton, Jill Lublin, Gerald Rogers, and MANY other amazing world leaders who want to change the world! We also appreciate their friendly and patient assistants, especially Perizae, Alice, Kristine, Jesse, and Leanne…kindness at its best.

Barbi, our editor, did an incredible job with our words, so our readers could read—and feel—the message that is in our hearts.

Debra Gano's beautiful words warmed our hearts, and we are excited to share a mission to let children know they are unique, beautiful, and valuable. Thank you so much!

We want to thank our friends Toria, Brianna, Emmy, Maddy, Samantha (and her sweet little sisters), Ella, Danielle (and her little sisters), Elyssa, Yulia, Delaney, Addison, Peyton, Kate, Talia, Lexi K., Rana, Ian, Nico, Daniella, Gigi, Robin, Alexus, Emma, Luke, and all of our friends.

Thank you to Diane Cunningham for letting us speak at her conference and inspiring us.

And of course, we are especially grateful to our awesome publishing team at Morgan James: David Hancock, Rick Frishman, Bethany, Margo, Bruce, Cindy, and Jim. What a great job they have done to bring our dream to reality and to help us get it out to the world.

Lastly, we would like to thank YOU for reading our book and for spreading the word!

Our hearts are full. Thank YOU!

About Elisha

Elisha is a homeschooled 11-year-old, and a passionate author, artist, kidpreneur, and speaker. She loves to write, read, spell, draw, paint, play basketball, and to play the piano and the guitar.

She is bilingual and speaks Spanish, English, and a little bit of Mandarin Chinese. She is proud to be a Certified Guerrilla Marketing Practitioner, trained by Jay Conrad Levinson himself.

Her greatest desire is to become a world-known artist, author, speaker, and entrepreneur. She hopes to someday get married in the temple and have children.

If she had only 3 words to describe herself they would be: creative, generous, and humorous. Elisha lives in Dallas, TX with her family and she loves spending time with them.

The people Elisha most admires are her mom, her baby sister, Eliana, and her sister Elyssa.

She feels that when she is painting or reading, she can be more imaginative. She prefers actually *feeling* what she is doing through paying attention to the emotion.

Elisha describes herself as a naïve artist by nature, yet she loves to explore new styles. Her favorite colors to work with are soft pastels, such as blue or pink. She especially loves to paint or draw nature and families.

She wrote I Love ME! at age 10, because she is passionate about helping other kids become bully-proof, love themselves, and be the best they can be.

About Elyssa

Elyssa is 10 years old. She enjoys being an entrepreneur, speaker, author, artist, and coach. She is homeschooled, and her favorite subjects in school are language arts, social studies, and art. Her greatest coach and mentor is her mom, Elayna Fernandez.

She plays the guitar and piano, but would also like to learn the ocarina, flute, and violin. She loves to play with her sister, dance ballet, draw, read, write stories, play tennis, and bike.

Elyssa was born in San Diego, California, and later moved to Naples, Florida with her single mother and her older sister. She now lives in Irving, Texas with her family.

She's fascinated with nature, especially animals, and to avoid hurting them, she became vegan. Her favorite colors are magenta, violet, and turquoise.

Elyssa likes planning ahead so she can be prepared. She has a dry-erase board for her schedule and she also has her daily tasks and expectations, responsibilities, and a fitness log. She describes herself as straight to the point, loves goals, and enjoys challenges.

Elyssa loves serving others and is very innovative. She teaches children to love themselves and have self-confidence through her books, blog posts, and artistic expressions.

Elyssa's desire is to help families grow together in unity and love and to help children all around the world have self-esteem. She has a testimony God loves her and all those around her, and wants to spread that message around the world!

She is almost always seen with her nose in a book, because she says it helps her learn, be observant, and exercise her imagination. Elyssa is bilingual in English and Spanish fluently.

Elyssa would be thrilled to get to know you. You can connect with her and her sister, Elisha, at WhollyART.com

About
WhollyART

Elisha and Elyssa are sisters, artists, authors, speakers and co-founders of WhollyART.

Their mission is to teach kids and tweens wholesome, positive values through art. Elisha and Elyssa have been mentored by world-renowned experts, featured in broadcast and print media and art galleries, and have even won awards!

"We don't just paint pretty pictures—we create guidelines for a better, happier life."

Elyssa *Elisha*

Questions? Comments? Testimonials?

Visit www.WhollyART.com

www.Facebook.com/WhollyART

www.Twitter.com/WhollyART

www.LinkedIn.com/WhollyART

Printed in the USA
CPSIA information can be obtained
at www.ICGtesting.com
JSHW050041300424
62140JS00017B/501